# A

# Apple Blossom

B

Bugle

C

Columbine

D

Double Daisy

# E

Eyebright

F

Fuchsia

G

Gorse

# H

## Herb Twopence

I

Iris

J

Jasmine

K

Kingcup

L

Lily-of-the-Valley

M

Mallow

N

Nasturtium

Orchis

P

Pansy

Q

Queen of the Meadow

Ragged Robin

**S**

Strawberry

T

Thrift

UV

Vetch

Wallflower

XY

Yellow Deadnettle

Z

Zinnia